US TACTICAL
AIR POWER
EUROPE 1942–1945

1

2

US TACTICAL AIR POWER
EUROPE 1942–1945

ROGER A. FREEMAN

ARMS AND
ARMOUR

1. The first official USAAF combat operation from the UK was flown on 4 July 1942, with four crews of the 15th Bomb Squadron (Light) participating with No 226 Squadron, RAF, in a low-level attack on airfields in the Netherlands. For his part in the operation and for bringing home a badly damaged Boston, Captain Charles Kegelman received the Distinguished Service Order – the second highest US decoration for bravery. At the investiture, a week after the action, the other three members of his crew received the Distinguished Flying Cross. They were Sgts Ben Cunningham and Robert Golay on the left and Lt Randall Dorton on the right of Kegelman.

2. For its first operations the 15th Bomb Squadron borrowed Douglas Bostons from the RAF's No 226 Squadron. In August 1942 the 15th BS received 16 Boston IIIs from the British as 'permanent' equipment and with these aircraft moved to North Africa in November. While based at Molesworth the squadron's personnel were introduced to the British afternoon tea ritual by the YMCA mobile cafeteria. The air and ground crews of 'Texas', 'K-King', serial AL445, taste the brew.

3. Paratroops in ground practice drop from a C-47 of the 60th Troop Carrier Group at Aldermaston, October 1942. The 8th Air Force received three troop carrier groups – the 60th, 62nd and 64th – equipped with C-47s and C-53s. These, with all other tactical flying units, were transferred to the newly formed 12th Air Force in September 1942. The 12th Air Force supported Operation 'Torch' in November 1942 and all its units in the UK had moved to North Africa by January 1943.

4. The 67th Reconnaissance Group arrived in Britain in September 1942 without aircraft. It was the only tactical fighter and reconnaissance unit assigned to the 8th Air Force after the departure of the 12th Air Force. Three of its squadrons were equipped with Spitfire Vs and a fourth with a mixture of L-4 Cubs, Bostons and A-20B Havocs. Although there were individual sorties in company with RAF units, the Group did not officially enter combat while with the 8th AF. In this photo a mixed formation of 12th and 109th Tac Rec Sqn Spitfires (marked 'ZM' and 'VX' respectively) are seen near their base at Membury.

Arms and Armour Press
A Cassell Imprint
Villiers House, 41–47 Strand, London WC2N 5JE.

Distributed in the USA by Sterling Publishing Co. Inc., 387 Park Avenue South, New York, NY 10016–8810.

Distributed in Australia by Capricorn Link (Australia) Pty. Ltd, P.O. Box 665, Lane Cove, New South Wales 2066.

British Library Cataloguing in Publication Data
Freeman, Roger A. (Roger Anthony) 1928–
US Tactical airpower: Europe 1942–1945
1. United States. Air Force. Military aircraft, history
I. Title
623.7460973
ISBN 1-85409-042-9

Designed and edited by DAG Publications Ltd. Designed by David Gibbons; edited by David Dorrell; layout by Anthony A. Evans; typeset by Ronset Typesetters Ltd, Darwen, Lancashire; camerawork by M&E Reproductions, North Fambridge, Essex; printed and bound in Great Britain by The Alden Press, Oxford.

Introduction

In the Second World War offensive air power came to be defined as strategic or tactical. The former was, broadly, assault on an enemy's war industry; the latter support of ground forces. In practice strategic air commands were often involved in tactical attacks and tactical air commands sometimes conducted what would be classed as strategic operations, a case of meeting demand with available forces.

The USAAF despatched a whole range of air units to the United Kingdom during the second half of 1942. Initially all were under the European Theatre of Operations (ETO) command designated 8th Air Force with a tentative commitment to support an invasion of continental Europe. This was soon replaced by an intention to invade North Africa later that year and the tactical units of the 8th Air Force were transferred to a new command, the 12th Air Force. After the 12th departed for Morocco and Algeria, the 8th Air Force's main preoccupation was strategic bombing, but it began rebuilding its tactical component under VIII Air Support Command. The flying units consisted of a single tactical reconnaissance group and a half-strength troop carrier group, operating in training and theatre support roles, respectively. In the spring of 1943 four B-26 Marauder groups arrived and after disastrous experience with the type under strategic direction, the Marauders were transferred to VIII Air Support Command. With revised tactics Marauder bombing operations became very successful.

With the Allied commitment to stage a cross-Channel invasion during the spring of 1944, the USAAF decided to form a separate tactical air force to support this venture. The redundant 9th Air Force in North Africa was resurrected in the UK and VIII Air Support Command was used as the operational nucleus. Eventually, the new 9th Air Force became in many respects as large as the 8th Air Force and at peak strength had more than 40,000 personnel and over 4,000 aircraft. The principal fighter-bomber for ground attack in support of the armies was the P-47 Thunderbolt, of which there were ultimately 45 squadrons in the 9th Air Force. Forty-four squadrons of B-26 Marauders and A-20 Havocs provided the medium and light bomber element, but both types were being replaced by A-26 Invaders towards the end of hostilities. A total of 56 troop carrier squadrons of IX Troop Carrier Command served airborne forces and hauled supplies with C-47 Skytrains. However, in August 1944 IX Troop Carrier Command came under the control of the 1st Allied Airborne Army. Following the invasion of southern France and the establishment of the 1st Tactical Air Force (Provisional), three 9th Air Force P-47 groups joined that organization, which was composed largely of 12th Air Force and French units from the Mediterranean theatre. However, the groups concerned were still viewed as being assigned to the 9th Air Force by USAAF Headquarters.

This Fotofax covers the story of United States tactical air power in the ETO from 1942 through to the victory in May 1945, providing the reader with a pictorial survey of aircraft and personalities.

Roger A. Freeman

Note: Aircraft listed is principal type used. TRS used -6. PRS used F-5. Unit Abbreviations: FS = Fighter Squadron, NFS = Night Fighter Squadron, BS = Bomb Squadron, TRS = Tactical Reconnaissance Squadron, PRS = Photographic Reconnaissance Squadron, NPS = Night Photographic Squadron, PFS = Pathfinder Squadron, TCS = Troop Carrier Squadron and LS = Liaison Squadron.

5. In March and April 1943 the first two squadrons of the 322nd Bomb Group arrived with Martin B-26B-2, -3 and -4 model Marauders. From their base at Bury St Edmunds, Suffolk, these units flew very low-level training missions for a number of weeks, preparing for hit-and-run operations against selected targets within the Marauder's range. B-26B-2 41-17993, seen over the Suffolk countryside, was wrecked when it hit the ground near Cambridge.

6. The first Marauder combat mission was flown against Ijmuiden power station in Holland on 14 May 1943. The CO of the 322nd BG briefed his crews for target identification using a sand table model – he is seen with pointer in hand.

7. The twelve B-26s despatched found their target but encountered heavy anti-aircraft fire. Many aircraft were hit and seven crewmen wounded. B-26 41-17988 was so badly damaged that the crew had to take to their parachutes over home base. Sadly the aircraft went out of control before the pilot could leave and he was killed in the ensuing crash. In this photo the wreck burns in a field at Rougham while Group personnel keep away from exploding ammunition.

8. A second low-level mission to Ijmuiden was flown on 17 May 1943 and all ten Marauders entering enemy airspace failed to return. These were B-26B 4 models with the original short wing and small ta[il]

8

assembly, like this example which was originally scheduled for the raid but could not be made fully serviceable in time.

9. A second Marauder group, the 323rd BG, had arrived in the UK by this time. Like the 322nd, it was trained for low-level attack. Moreover, it was equipped with the special B-26C-6 model which dispensed with a co-pilot and had special modifications. Externally the 'C-6 was very similar to the later B-26Bs with increased wing span, larger empennage and twelve .50in machine-guns. The photograph shows B-26C-6 41-34709 after take-off from Earls Colne, the 323rd's operational base.

9

10. Low-level attack was abandoned and the Marauders were transferred from VIII Bomber Command to VIII Air Support Command. For several weeks they were non-operational while new tactics were developed. In late July 1943 medium-altitude missions were commenced, emulating the formations of the US heavy bombers. With RAF Spitfire escort, these operations proved very successful. Here 322nd BG Marauders taxi to the runway at their new base at Great Saling, Essex. B-26B-10 'Pickled-Dilly', 41-18276, survived 105 missions before being lost to a night fighter in July 1944.

11. Two more Marauder groups, the 386th and 387th BGs, had arrived in June and July and soon joined the 322nd and 323rd in medium-level bombing, the total force of operational B-26s then being some 250. During the first three months of operations losses were only 0.3 per cent of sorties, in part due to fighter escort, usually RAF Spitfires but sometimes USAAF P-47 Thunderbolts. Here a 78th FG P-47 accompanies 322nd BG Marauders.

12. Although the Marauder was no longer used for low-level attack it still retained its fixed forward-firing armament of five .50in Brownings, four in side blisters and one firing through the right side of the nose Plexiglas. These weapons were sighted and fired by the pilot. Additional forward firepower was provided by the flexible .50in gun for use by the bombardier. The aircraft in the photograph is not equipped with a bombsight.

13

14

15

16

13, 14, 15, 16, 17 and 18. Marauder nose decoraions and nicknames were as colourful and sexist as those on the big American bombers. In this selection: 'Our Baby' was 41-31603 'AN:Q' of the 553rd BS, 386th BG; 'Hell's Fury', 41-31625, 'YA:R' of the 555th BS, 386th BG; 'Impatient Virgin II', 41-34951, 'SS:P' of the 451st BS, 322nd BG; 'Klassie Lassie', 41-31944, 'WT:G' of the 456th BS, 323rd BG; 'Heavenly Body', 41-31664, 'KX:A' of the 558th BS, 387th BG; and 'Sky Queen', 41-35264, 'TQ:U' of the 559th BS, 387th BG.

17

18

19. The bomb bay of a B-26 accommodated almost as large a load as that of a B-17 and 4,000lb loads could be hauled to targets 200 miles from their bases. Here 386th BG armourers steady a 500lb HE bomb as it is winched into a bay. A release shackle is already fixed to the two bomb lugs.

20. Even the Nissen huts were named on this Boxted site. B-26 pilots 2/Lt Tom Hillman (left) and 1/Lt John Miller attempt to master the personal transport of the time.

21. On 15 October 1943 HQ 9th Air Force was established in the UK at Sunninghill Park, using the staff of VIII Air Support Command. The 3rd Bomb Wing at Marks Hall, Essex, became IX Bomber Command. The redesignations did not affect Marauder operations but later in October group identification markings were introduced. These took the form of coloured tail bands, such as those sported by 'Hangover Hut', 41-31694, 'FW:F' of the 387th BG (yellow with black diagonal stripes) and 'Elmer', 41-31577, 'AN:Y' of the 553rd BS, 386th BG (yellow), seen after bombing Leeuwarden airfield in Holland.

22. Two weeks after its establishment in the UK the 9th Air Force received its first fighter group, the 354th, which was also the first to be equipped with the new P-51B Mustang. Earlier Mustang models had been used chiefly for ground support and the

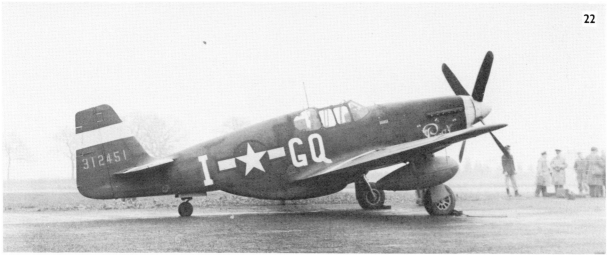

new Packard Merlin-powered version was also at first expected to serve in a similar capacity. However, the P-51Bs were immediately assigned to escort heavy bombers of the 8th Air Force as the fighters' 400-mile radius of action on internal fuel made them far superior for the task than either the P-47 or P-38. The 354th P-51Bs quickly proved their worth, as with two 75-US-gallon drop tanks – the type under the wing of 'Peggy' – they could accompany the bombers to their furthest targets.

23

23. The personal Mustang (43-12410, 'GQ:M') of 1/Lt Charles F. Gumm at Boxted airfield. Gumm was originally credited as the first Mustang ace, but re-assessment of claims gave this honour to two fellow 354th Group pilots, Don Beerbower and Jack Bradley.

24. Flying a bomber escort from Boxted on 11 January 1944, Major James H. Howard, CO of the 356th FS, 354th FG, was involved in an action that later brought him the only Medal of Honor (highest US award for bravery) to be won by a US fighter pilot in the European Theatre of Operations. He is seen here in his personal P-51B (43-6315), nicknamed 'Ding Hao'. Howard had previously served with the American Volunteer Group in China/Burma and the US Marines – hence the symbols for Japanese victories. This P-51B has been fitted with a Malcolm sliding cockpit canopy.

25. The tactical reconnaissance squadrons of the 67th Reconnaissance Group eventually re-equipped with Mustangs when these became available. Meanwhile it

24

soldiered on with Spitfires. The narrow undercarriage track was a frequent cause of landing accidents. This 15th TRS aircraft succumbed at Duxford.

26. Two other P-51B groups were assigned to the 9th Air Force in England, but one was exchanged for a P-47 group with the 8th Air Force and the other had its mission changed to tactical reconnaissance. Three P-38 Lightning groups were also assigned to the 9th Air Force but the main fighter type was the redoubtable P-47D Thunderbolt, of which a total of thirteen groups were on hand by May 1944. The first of these began operations in February 1944, initially with fighter sweeps and bomber escorts, but gradually going over to the bombing and strafing of ground targets. Clutching a 250lb bomb under each wing rack and a 108-US-gallon drop tank below the belly, 'Princess Pat' (42-76542, 'B2:W') of the 366th FG waits to be flagged off at Thruxton for a dive-bombing raid. This P-47 was shot down soon after D-Day.

27. Fighter groups that arrived in the UK after the spring of 1944 were equipped predominantly with aircraft devoid of camouflage paint. This example is a P-47D (42-26061, '6V:E') of the 53rd FS, 36th FG, at Kingsnorth landing ground. Squadron personnel are examining flak damage following a ground-attack mission.

28. Four more B-26 groups were sent to the 9th Air Force during the early months of 1944 – the 344th based at Stansted, the 391st at Matching, the 394th at Boreham and the 397th at Rivenhall, all in Essex county, as were the older B-26 groups. Mechanics of the 497th BS, 344th BG, are seen checking over a Marauder after one of the unit's early operations. The B-26 proved to be a demanding aircraft for maintenance but a very reliable performer.

29. At IX Bomber Command's Essex airfields the accommodation for both air and ground crews was the ubiquitous Nissen hut and personal transport cycles supplied by the British. This is a bike parking lot on a living site at Andrewsfield (Great Saling). [*Photo: E. Allen*]

30 and 31. Although the Marauders continued to turn in the lowest loss per sortie rate of any Allied medium or heavy bomber operating from the UK, their crews regularly had to face accurate and intensive 'flak'. Here a 386th BG aircraft suffers a direct hit in the wing, igniting fuel. In the second photo the wing has burned off and the bomber falls out of control. This occurred while Marauders were attacking V-1 flying bomb sites in the Pas de Calais, a frequent objective during the winter of 1943–44.

32. On occasions B-26s fell foul of enemy fighters. 'Lorraine II' (41-31746, 'ER:K') of the 450th BS, 322nd BG, took a blasting from cannon shells and bullets but survived to fly and fight again. One shell has passed completely through the fuselage without exploding.

33. To complete its complement IX Bomber Command received three groups equipped with Douglas A-20 Havocs. These were the 409th BG based at Little Walden, the 410th BG based at Gosfield and the 416th BG at Wethersfield. The 416th was the first to become operational – in March 1944. The main model was the A-20G which had a 'solid' nose sporting six .50in-calibre machine-guns for ground strafing and twin .50s in a dorsal power turret for defence, as on this example, 43-9182, '5H:B', assigned to the 668th BS, 416th BG.

34. The other model was the A-20J which was similar to the A-20G except that it had a 'bombardier nose' in place of the fixed armament. A-20Js were used as formation lead aircraft and carried a bombardier and Norden sight. Although the A-20G was intended for low-level attack, the 9th Air Force Havocs were employed in similar fashion to the B-26s, in medium altitude, drop-on-leader formation bombing. In the photograph, A-20J '2A:W' is seen leading a 416th BG formation of A-20Gs.

34

35. After the P-47 the most prolific aircraft in the 9th Air Force by the spring of 1944 was the Douglas C-47 Skytrain – of which there were nearly 1,000 in fourteen troop carrier groups based at airfields in the south-west of England and Lincolnshire in the east. One of the first groups to arrive in the UK was the 435th TCG – 42-92098 ('SH:C') shown here was a C-47A assigned to the Group's 75th TCS.

35

36

36. Most 9th Air Force squadrons were identified by code letter or number/letter combinations. C-47s were unusual in having these painted on either side of the nose. This example is the '90' code of the 85th TCS.

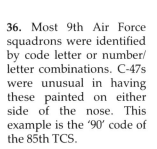

37

38

37. On 8 May 1944, the 322nd BG's 'Mild and Bitter' became the first Marauder flying from the UK to complete 100 missions. The veteran, officially 41-31819, 'DR:X', was 'autographed' by 322nd personnel before being flown back to the United States.

38. During the 12 hours preceding the launch of the cross-Channel invasion on 6 June 1944 all 9th Air Force combat aircraft were painted with distinctive black and white identification bands, which became known as D-Day Stripes. 'Silver' P-47D 42-25857

served with the 507th FS, 404th FG, a unit which contributed to the 4,700-plus sorties flown by the 9th Air Force that day. [*Dan Morse*]

39. Only nine 9th Air Force fighter-bombers were lost on D-Day from over 2,000 sorties. P-47 42-75197 of the 365th FG was damaged by blast from the bomb its pilot released at low level, but he managed to nurse the aircraft back for a crash-landing at Beaulieu.

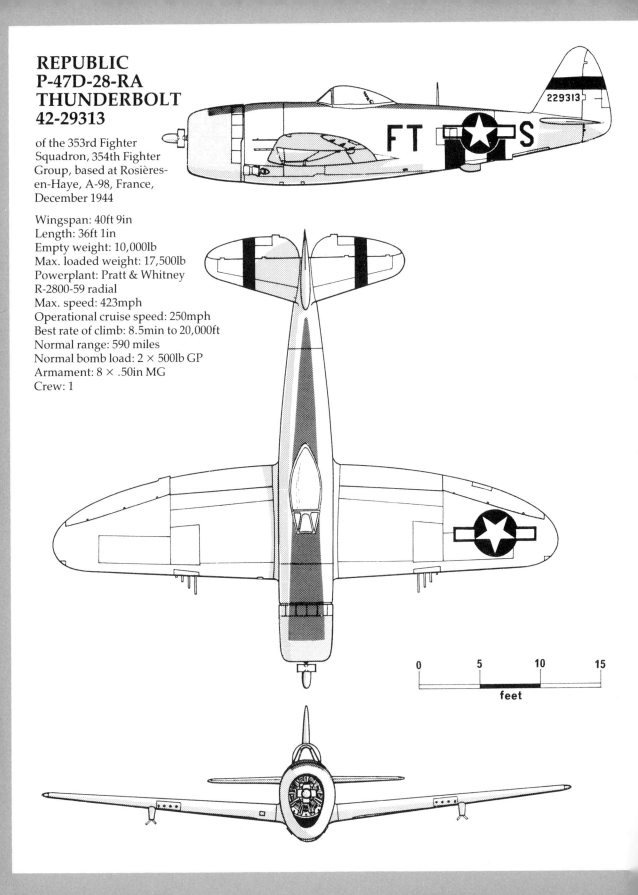

REPUBLIC
P-47D-28-RA
THUNDERBOLT
42-29313

of the 353rd Fighter
Squadron, 354th Fighter
Group, based at Rosières-
en-Haye, A-98, France,
December 1944

Wingspan: 40ft 9in
Length: 36ft 1in
Empty weight: 10,000lb
Max. loaded weight: 17,500lb
Powerplant: Pratt & Whitney
R-2800-59 radial
Max. speed: 423mph
Operational cruise speed: 250mph
Best rate of climb: 8.5min to 20,000ft
Normal range: 590 miles
Normal bomb load: 2 × 500lb GP
Armament: 8 × .50in MG
Crew: 1

229313

FT S

0   5   10   15

feet

MARTIN
B-26G-25-MA
MARAUDER 44-68118

of the 585th Bomb Squadron, 394th
Bomb Group, based at
Cambrai/ Niergnies, A-74,
France, March 1945

Wingspan: 71ft
Length: 56ft 1in
Empty weight: 23,700lb
Max. loaded weight: 38,200lb
Powerplant: 2 × Pratt & Whitney R-
2800-43 radials
Max. speed: 277mph
Operational cruise speed: 195mph
Best rate of climb: 24min to 15,000ft
Normal range: 1,150 miles
Normal bomb load: 4,000lb
Armament: 12 × .50in MG
Crew: 7

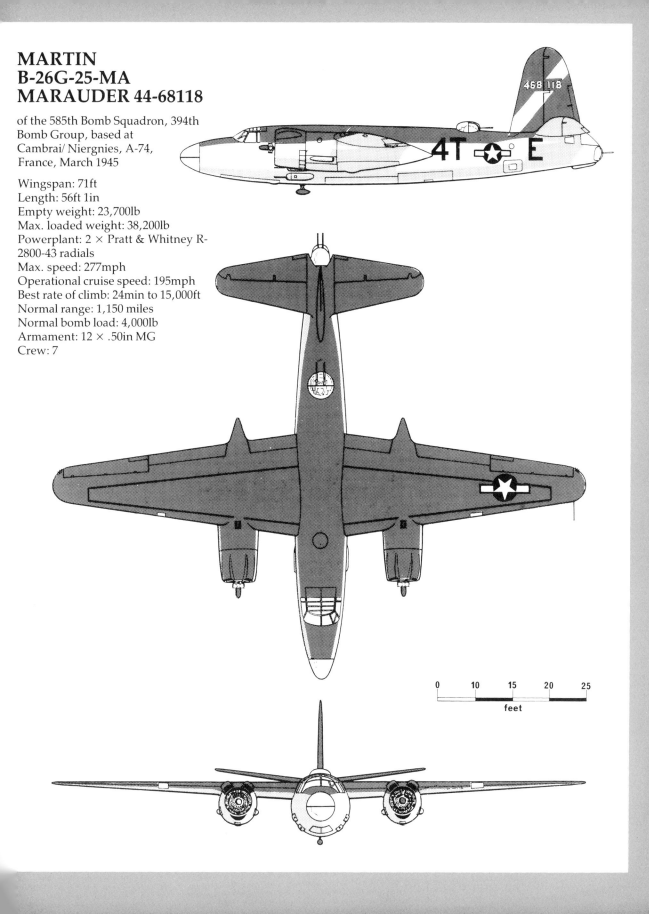

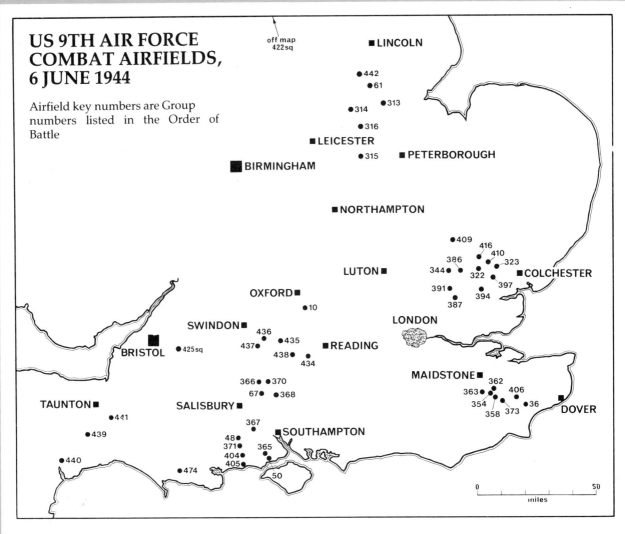

US 9TH AIR FORCE COMBAT AIRFIELDS, 6 JUNE 1944

US 9TH AIR FORCE ORDER OF BATTLE, 6 JUNE 1944

IX FIGHTER COMMAND

422nd NFS	P-61	Scorton
425th NFS	P-61	Charmy Down

IX TAC

67th TRG	F-5/F-6	Middle Wallop

70th Fighter Wing

48th FG	P-47D	Ibsley
367th FG	P-38J	Stoney Cross
371st FG	P-47D	Bisterne
474th FG	P-38J	Warmwell

71st Fighter Wing

366th FG	P-47D	Thruxton

368th FG	P-47D	Chilbolton
370th FG	P-38J	Andover

84th Fighter Wing

50th FG	P-47D	Lymington
365th FG	P-47D	Beaulieu
404th FG	P-47D	Winkton
405th FG	P-47D	Christchurch

XIX TAC

10th PG	F-5/F-6	Chalgrove

100th Fighter Wing

354th FG	P-51B/D	Lashenden
358th FG	P-47D	High Halden

362nd FG	P-47D	Headcorn
363rd FG	P-51B/D	Staplehurst

303rd Fighter Wing

36th FG	P-47D	Kingsnorth
373rd FG	P-47D	Woodchurch
406th FG	P-47D	Ashford

IX BOMBER COMMAND

1st PF Sqn (P)	B-26B/C	Andrewsfield

97th Combat Bomb Wing

409th BG	A-20G/J	Little Walden
410th BG	A-20G/J	Gosfield

416th BG	A-20G/J	Wethersfield

98th Combat Bomb Wing

323rd BG	B-26B/C	Earls Colne
387th BG	B-26B/C	Chipping Ongar
394th BG	B-26B/C	Boreham
397th BG	B-26B/C	Rivenhall

99th Combat Bomb Wing

322nd BG	B-26B/C	Andrewsfield
344th BG	B-26B/C	Stansted
386th BG	B-26B/C	Great Dunmow
391st BG	B-26B/C	Matching

IX TROOP CARRIER COMMAND

50th Troop Carrier Wing

439th TCG	C-47	Upottery
440th TCG	C-47	Exeter
441st TCG	C-47	Merryfield
442nd TCG	C-47	Fulbeck

52nd Troop Carrier Wing

61st TCG	C-47	Barkeston
313th TCG	C-47	Folkingham
314th TCG	C-47	Saltby
315th TCG	C-47	Spanhoe
316th TCG	C-47	Cottesmore

53rd Troop Carrier Wing

434th TCG	C-47	Aldermaston
435th TCG	C-47	Welford
436th TCG	C-47	Membury
437th TCG	C-47	Ramsbury
438th TCG	C-47	Greenham Common

(Aircraft models listed were principal equipment)

US 9TH AIR FORCE ORDER OF BATTLE, 8 MAY 1945

IX TACTICAL AIR COMMAND

36th FG
22, 23, 53 FS	P-47D	Kassel/Rothwesten	R-12

365th FG
386, 387, 388 FS	P-47D	Fritzlar	Y-86

404th FG
506, 507, 508 FS	P-47D	Fritzlar	Y-86

474th FG
428, 429, 430 FS	P-38	Langensalza	R-2

67th TRG
107 TRS, 109 TRS, 30 PRS	F-6, F-5	Eschwege	R-11
422 NFS	P-61	Langensalza	R-2

XIX TACTICAL AIR COMMAND

48th FG
492, 493, 494 FS	P-47D	Illesheim	R-10

354th FG
353, 355, 356 FS	P-51D	Ansbach	R-45

362nd FG
377, 378, 379 FS	P-47D	Illesheim	R-10

367th FG
392, 393, 394 FS	P-47D	Eschborn	Y-74

368th FG
395, 396, 397 FS	P-47D	Frankfurt-am-Main	Y-73

371st FG
404, 405, 406 FS	P-47D	Furth	R-30

405th FG
509, 510, 511 FS	P-47D	Kitzingen	R-6

9th TRG (P)
9 WRS, 31 TRS, 39 PRS, 155 NPS	F-6, F-5, A-20	Wiesbaden	Y-80

10th PRG
12 TRS, 15 TRS,	F-6,	Furth	

162 TRS, 31 PRS	F-5		R-30
425 NFS	P-61	Furth	R-30

XXIX TACTICAL AIR COMMAND

366th FG
389, 390, 391 FS	P-47D	Munster/Handorf	Y-94

370th FG
401, 402, 403 FS	P-51D	Gutersloh	Y-99

373rd FG
410, 411, 412 FS	P-47D	Lippstadt	Y-98

406th FG
512, 513, 514 FS	P-47D	Munster/Handorf	Y-94

363rd TRG
160 TRS, 161 TRS, 33, PRS	F-6, F-5	Brunswick	R-37

1ST TACTICAL AIR FORCE

50th FG
10, 81, 313 FS	P-47D	Giebelstadt	Y-90

358th FG
365, 366, 367 FS	P-47D	Sandhofen	Y-79

69th TRG
10 TRS, 22 TRS, 111 TRS, 34PRS	F-6, F-5	Haguenau	Y-39

(1st TAF also had P-47 and B-26 groups that were assigned to the 12th Air Force)

9TH BOMB DIVISION

97th Bomb Wing

409th BG
640, 641, 642, 643 BS	A-26	Laon/Couvron	A-70

410th BG

644, 645, 646, 647 BS	A-20 & A-26	Juvincourt	A-68
416th BG			
668, 669, 670, 671 BS	A-26	Laon/Athies	A-69

98th Bomb Wing
323rd BG

453, 454, 455, 456 BS	B-26	Denain/Prouvy	A-83
387th BG			
556, 557, 558, 559 BS	B-26	Maastricht	Y-44
394th BG			
584, 585, 586, 587 BS	B-26	Venlo	Y-55
397th BG			

| 596, 597, 598, 599 BS | B-26 | Venlo | Y-55 |
| 1st PFS (P) | B-26 | Venlo | Y-55 |

99th Bomb Wing
322nd BG

449, 450, 451, 452 BS	B-26	Le Culot	A-89
344th BG			
494, 495, 496, 497 BS	B-26	Florennes/Juzaine	A-78
386th BG			
552, 553, 554, 555 BS	A-26	St Trond	A-92
391st BG			
572, 573, 574, 575 BS	A-26	Asch	Y-29
1st PFS (P)	B-26	Asch	Y-29

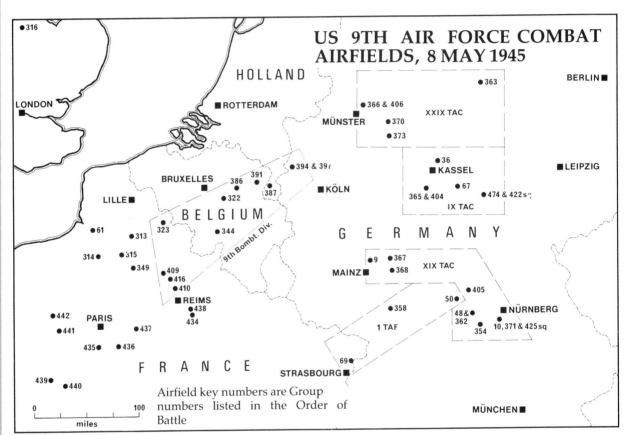

US 9TH AIR FORCE COMBAT AIRFIELDS, 8 MAY 1945

Airfield key numbers are Group numbers listed in the Order of Battle

IX TROOP CARRIER COMMAND

50th Troop Carrier Wing
439th TCG

| 91, 92, 93, 94 TCS | C-47 | Chateaudun | A-39 |

440th TCG

| 95, 96, 97, 98 TCS | C-47 | Orleans/Bricy | A-50 |

441st TCG

| 99, 100, 301, 302 TCS | C-47 | Dreux | A-41 |

442nd TCG

| 303, 304, 305, 306 TCS | C-47 | St Andre-de-l'Eure | B-24 |

52nd Troop Carrier Wing
61st TCG

| 14, 15, 53, 59 TCS | C-47 | Abbeville | B-92 |

313th TCG

| 29, 47, 48, 49 TCS | C-46 | Achiet | B-54 |

314th TCG

| 32, 50, 61, 62 TCS | C-47 | Poix | B-44 |

315th TCG

| 34, 43, 309, 310 TCS | C-47 | Amiens/Glisy | B-48 |

316th TCG

| 36, 37, 44, 45 TCS | C-47 | Cottesmore | |

349th TCG

| 23, 312, 313, 314 TCS | C-46 | Roye/Amy | A-73 |

53rd Troop Carrier Wing

434th TCG				83, 84, 85, 86 TCS	C-47	Coulommiers	A-58
71, 72, 73, 74 TCS	C-47	Mourmelon-le-Grand	A-80	438th TCG			
435th TCG				87, 88, 89, 90 TCS	C-47	Prosnes	A-79
75, 76, 77, 78 TCS	C-47	Bretigny	A-48	112 LS	L-5	Buc	Y-4
436th TCG				125 LS	L-5	Brunswick	R-37
79, 80, 81, 82 TCS	C-47	Melun	A-55	153 LS	L-5	Weimar	R-7
437th TCG				158 LS	L-5	Ahrweiler	
				167 LS	L-5	Pfaffengrund	

40. P-38 Lightnings were selected to patrol over Allied shipping off Normandy on D-Day and for several weeks following. Their distinctive shape provided positive identification as a 'friendly' for naval anti-aircraft gunners whose aircraft recognition was notoriously bad. This P-38J seen banking over Avranches was an aircraft of the 394th FS, 367th FG.

41. Mechanics of the 81st FS, 50th FG, carrying paper plastic composition drop tanks at the unit's Lymington base. With a capacity of 108 US gallons, these tanks gave Thunderbolts several hours' endurance to patrol over the Allied beachhead. Both P-47Ds in the background were subsequently destroyed as a result of enemy action.

42. Men of the 816th Engineer Battalion laying square mesh tracking at A-3, Cardonville, the first US advanced landing ground to become operational in Normandy. A P-

47D of the 512th FS, 406th FG, is the nearest of those in the background.

43. First 9th Air Force group to move to France was the 368th FG whose first squadron took up residence at Cardonville on 16 June 1944 and commenced operational flights the next day.

44. A P-47 of the 492nd FS, 48th FG, being refuelled at A-4, Deux Jumeaux, where the unit moved on 18 June 1944. The pilot, Lt A. W. Martin, stands on the wing with mechanics. The surfaces of parking areas were compacted soil.

45

45. Assigned to and operated by various US Army units, notably signals and artillery companies, the Piper L-4 Grasshopper was a familiar sight over the Allied lines in France. The fuselage numerals were the unit's code identification.

46. The predominant type in IX Troop Carrier Command was the C-47 Skytrain but there were also a few C-53D Skytroopers. The principal difference was the rear fuselage airliner-type entrance door of the latter. This Skytrooper, 42-68835, 'CU:W', was operated by the 72nd TCS, 434th TCG, which was based at Aldermaston in 1944.

47. Having dropped paratroops on D-Day, IX Troop Carrier Command C-47s and C-53s were soon kept busy hauling cargo to French airfields. Aircraft of the 435th and 437th TCGs appear in this line-up.

48. A new shape that appeared in western Europe in May 1944 and became operational early in July was the Northrop P-61 Black Widow. With a twin-boom configuration like the P-38's, the P-61 was the first purpose-built night fighter in the USAAF. The 9th Air Force had two squadrons, the 422nd and 425th NFSs, neither assigned to a group. Early P-61s of the 422nd NFS, like 42-5535 seen at Hurn, arrived in standard olive drab and grey finish but were later given an all-gloss black finish.

46

47

48

49. In the summer of 1944 the short-range bomb load of A-20 Havocs was increased by the addition of a rack under each wing. A 500lb bomb could be carried on each, increasing the load to 3,000lb. A-20G 43-10158 '6Q:'V' of the 647th BS, 410th BG, carries this load en route to a target in France.

50. The P-47 workhorses generally carried out ground-attack using 500lb bombs and by strafing, but in the late summer of 1944 air-to-ground rockets were introduced. Six 4.5in rockets were carried in six infantry type launch tubes clustered in threes under each wing. Although the missile was very effective against armoured vehicles, it did not find favour with the majority of P-47 pilots due to difficulty in achieving accurate aim.

51. By mid-June some of the new 'Superbolts' – unofficial nickname of the P-47D-25 model – were received in 9th Air Force groups. These had a number of improvements, notably greater internal fuel capacity and a 'bubble' canopy allowing the pilot all-round vision. One of the first in the 373rd FG was used by deputy CO, Lt Col Don Bennink, seen at the unit's base, A-29 St James, after returning from a mission.

52

53

52. Ground-attack was a hazardous task and enemy ground fire claimed many US fighters. The Thunderbolt was a sturdy aircraft and pilots of stricken machines were often able to make a crash-landing and survive. This P-47D-28, 42-28474 of the 23rd FS, 36th FG, came to grief near Dijon where it attracted attention from the local farming community.

53. CO of the 365th FG, Col Ray Stecker had a lucky escape when his flight was attacked from above by a strong force of Bf 109s. In diving to evade, his aircraft was hit by ground fire, two shells exploding in the fuselage just behind his seat.

54. Deputy CO of the 365th FG, Lt Col John R. Murphy at one time carried a screamer whistle on his P-47 with the idea of increasing the concern of enemy troops under attack. The device was an adaptation of a German incendiary shell.

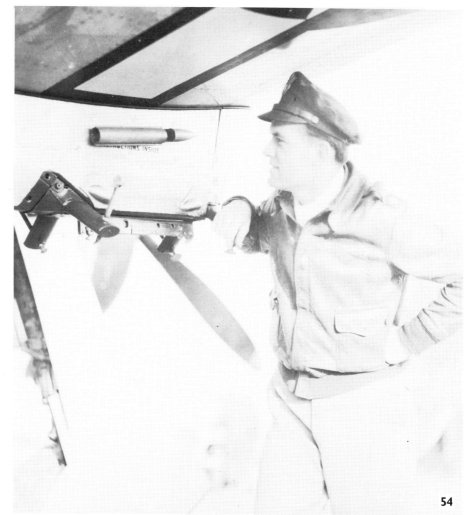

55. A 485th FS, 370th FG, P-38J, 44-23520, '7F:O', gathers speed on the Cardonville strip. Even spraying waste oil on the compacted soil runways did not prevent every take-off raising a cloud of dust in the July sun.

54

55

56.

56. In August 1944 IX Troop Carrier Command was transferred from the 9th Air Force to 1st Allied Airborne Army control, together with comparable RAF organizations. In mid-September Operations 'Market' and 'Garden' were staged, the airborne assault to secure bridges in the Low Countries. C-47 units were heavily involved in the delivery of paratroops and many towed assault gliders. The Waco CG-4A was the standard US assault glider and had a maximum combat payload of 3,750lb.

57.

57. An adaptation of a sea-search radar (SCR-717C) was installed in special pathfinder C-47s which acted as formation leaders so that drop points could be located accurately. The radar antenna was fixed to the nose below the cockpit, as on C-47 42-92099 of a pathfinder squadron.

58

58. By the autumn of 1944 some 40 P-61 Black Widows were operating in Europe from France on night fighter patrols. Gloss-black P-61A 42-5565 'Double Trouble' was the aircraft of Lt Robert Bolinder, seen flying in the vicinity of Southampton before the 422nd moved to the continent.

59. Lt Bolinder is the pilot of the 422nd NFS CO's aircraft in this photograph. The 'scoreboard' shows one enemy aircraft claim and 55 operational flights.

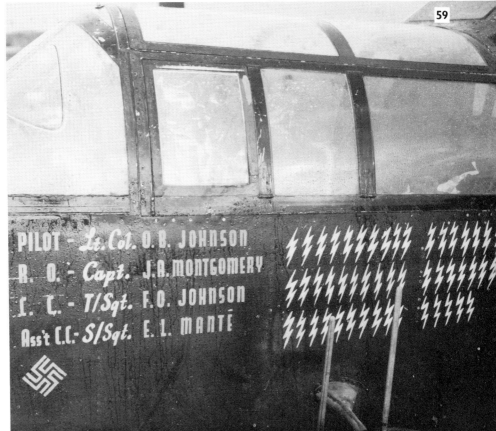

59

PILOT - *Lt. Col.* O. B. JOHNSON
R. O. - *Capt.* J. A. MONTGOMERY
F. T. - *T/Sgt.* F. O. JOHNSON
Ass't C.C. - *S/Sgt.* E. L. MANTÉ

60

60. Originally devised by the 8th Air Force, the modified P-38 known as the 'Droopsnoot', which allowed a bombardier and bombsight to be carried in the nose compartment, was taken up by 9th Air Force units. Among other duties, Droopsnoots were employed in leading P-38s for medium-altitude formation bombing. The operators of this example, the 474th FG, became the only fighter group in the 9th Air Force to retain the Lightning, the other two groups converting to P-47s and P-51s during the final months of hostilities.

61. The Lightning continued to be the principal aircraft used for tactical photographic reconnaissance. 'Heat Wave Hatty', 42-68290, was a veteran of the 34th PRS, photographed at Dijon. [*P. Gandillet*]

61

62. Bombardier's view of the French countryside through the nosepiece of a Droopsnoot. Note remote compass indicator and the photographer's shoes!

63. The winter of 1944–45 was particularly severe for western Europe, making both aircraft maintenance and operations difficult. These men are removing a heavy fall of snow from the tail of a C-47 operated by the 31st Air Transport Group of Air Service Command.

64. An attractive if chill scene at A-61 Beauvais/ Tille as the crew prepare to board 'Patricia Ann', B-26F, 43-34132, 'ER:Z' of the 450th BS, 322nd BG. The IX Bomber Command groups moved to the continent between late August and early October 1944.

65. On New Year's Day 1945 the Luftwaffe launched a mass low-level strafing raid on a number of British and American airfields. One of the worst hit was Metz/Frescaty, occupied by the 365th FG which had eighteen P-47s destroyed or badly damaged. This photograph, taken shortly after the attack, shows three Thunderbolts burning.

66. Early in 1945 IX Troop Carrier Command received 200 Curtiss C-46 Commando transports, a type with greater fuselage cargo capacity than the C-47. The 313th TCG converted to the type and the remainder equipped the 349th TCG which arrived in the UK in March. 'N3:O' was used by the 49th TCS of the 313th TCG.

67. C-46s of the 313th TCG on a training flight over France with a paratrooper about to leave the fuselage door. Both C-46 groups moved to the continent before the end of hostilities, as did all but one of IX Troop Carrier Command's C-47 groups.

68. The last major airborne assault of the war in which IX Troop Carrier Command aircraft were involved was the crossing of the Rhine on 24 March 1945. The paratroopers jumping from these 79th TCS, 436th TCG, C-47s were training.

69

69. The final production models of the Marauder, the B-26F and B-26G, began reaching 9th Air Force groups in the summer of 1944. The main difference between these and earlier models was the wing's angle of incidence which was increased by 3½° in the cause of shortening take-off and landing runs. The final production B-26Gs had camouflage paint re-introduced on the upper surface, as on 44-68161 'H9:Q' of the 586th BS, 394th BG.

70. The Marauder proved to be one of the most durable of all USAAF aircraft. Many of the B-26Bs that started operations in the summer of 1943 were still going strong at the end of the war and, like

70

71

72

'Smokey Joe' of the 456th BS, 323rd BG, had over 150 combat missions to their credit.

71. With B-26 and A-20 production being phased out, the proposed replacement type was the Douglas A-26 Invader. First examples were given a combat trial by a squadron of the 386th BG in the summer of 1944 and the 416th BG converted from A-20s to A-26s in November that year. These are aircraft of the 670th BS.

72. With the shrinking borders of enemy-held territory, so the concentration of flak increased. During an attack on communication targets at Munstereifel, Germany, an accurate barrage destroyed one 409th BG A-26. The flaming remains are to be seen below and behind another A-26B which has been hit in its right engine.

73

74

75

73 and 74. During the final months of hostilities many of the P-47 groups adopted colourful markings. P-47D 44-32793 'A7:J' of the 395th FS, 368th FG, has a yellow tail tip to identify the group and red cowling for the squadron. P-47D 44-33057 '4P:W' of the 513th FS, 406th FG, has a red cowling for the squadron identification and the group marking of red, blue and yellow horizontal tail bands.

75. In February 1945 the first Marauder group began full conversion to the A-26 Invader. The line-up on the Beaumont-sur-Oise runway includes several B-26s that had served the 386th BG since it entered combat.

76. In November 1944 the 1st Tactical Air Force (Provisional) was created to control those US and French air units supporting Allied armies that had invaded the French Mediterranean coast in September and were later deployed in the southern part of the front. Most of 1st TAF's flying units had come from the 12th Air Force in Italy and Corsica, but a few 9th Air Force reconnaissance squadrons and three P-47 groups were transferred to this command. The 50th FG P-47 being armed in this photograph had its cowling painted red, a marking that was common to all aircraft fighter aircraft serving 1st TAF.

77. Several 9th Air Force P-47 groups modified one or two P-47s as two-seaters for training and observation purposes. This example was the work of the 373rd FG.

78. Most successful fighter squadron in the whole USAAF was the 353rd FS of the 354th FG. The original Merlin Mustang squadron, it had credits of 289 enemy aircraft destroyed in air combat by VE-Day. Of its 19 fighter aces, Capt Ken Dahlberg, seen talking to his armourers, had 14 victories.

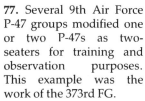

79. Similar to the L-4 Grasshopper, the Stinson L-5 Sentinel was the preferred type for artillery observation with many ground companies. This example served a US 7th Army unit. The Sentinel was also the primary equipment of the six liaison squadrons.

80. To maintain fuel supplies to Allied mechanized units, IX Troop Carrier Command flew gasoline to forward bases in France. In 1945 several B-24 heavy bombers had their armament removed and were fitted with fuselage fuel cells to become flying tankers under the designation C-109.

81. A demand for tactical reconnaissance intelligence by the ground forces led to the despatch of the 69th Reconnaissance Group to France in March 1945. Its component squadrons were equipped with F-6K Mustangs, the reconnaissance version of the P-51K. 'Rio Rita' carries the green identity tail markings of the 22nd TRS.

82. A 31st PRS F-5E wearing the white and blue checkerboard that identified aircraft of the 10th Photographic Group. Camera-equipped Lightnings were busy keeping watch over the German countryside for many weeks during the closing stages of the conflict and after VE-Day. [*A. P. Clarke*].

83. It is believed that the last enemy aircraft shot down by a US pilot was that which attacked Lt Robert C. Little when he was flying this F-6C Mustang of the 12th TRS, 10th PG, on 8 May 1945. Total 9th Air Force claims for air combat were 4,180 destroyed. Losses were nearly 3,000 aircraft of which 2,150 were fighters. A total of 1,529 men were known to have been killed in action and 1,910 were listed missing in action at this date. The ground attack claims of 9th Air Force units were prodigious: some 4,500 armoured fighting vehicles, 50,000 motor vehicles, 50,000 pieces of rolling stock, to list but a few. Combat sorties exceeded 368,500 for all types.